clarity & connection

Also by yung pueblo

inward

clarity & connection

yung pueblo

Andrews McMeel
PUBLISHING®

contents

all human beings
are united by
birth,
life,
death, and
every emotion
in between

the biggest shift in your life happens when you
go *inward*.
you step in and observe all that you find with
acceptance;
the love you bring lights up your self-awareness;
you start seeing how the past is packed into your
mind and heart—
patience, honesty, and observation start the
healing process.

with time, intention, and good healing practices,
the past loses its power over your life.
you continue the process—stepping in, feeling,
understanding, and letting go.
and then you start noticing the results; you are
not the same anymore.
your mind feels lighter and develops a new,
sharper *clarity*.
you start arriving into your life and relationships
ready for deeper *connection*.

self-awareness

heal yourself, but don't rush
help people, but have boundaries
love others, but don't let them harm you
love yourself, but don't become egotistical
stay informed, but don't overwhelm yourself
embrace change, but keep pursuing your goals

next time you feel agitated
because you are falling back into past patterns,
remember that simply being aware
that you are repeating the past
is a sign of progress

self-awareness comes before
the leap forward in
your personal transformation

it is not easy

healing yourself
building new habits
observing reality without projection or delusion

this is work that takes effort

but if you persist
the fruits of your labor will
have an immensely positive
impact on your life

maturity
is knowing that
when your mood is down
you should not trust
the way you see yourself

throw away the idea
that healing is forgetting

the real result is no longer
reacting to old triggers
with the same intensity as before

the memories are still there,
but they do not have the
same power over your mind

i spent years unaware
that i was running away from myself,
always seeking company or entertainment
so that i would not have to face
the dark clouds storming inside of me

every moment was an opportunity for diversion;
friendships were a means of escape,
pleasure a temporary relief from pain

i did not notice that my relationships were shallow
because of how far away i was from myself

i did not understand why solitude felt unbearable
and why "fun" could not permanently settle
turbulent emotions

for far too long i was unaware
that the only way for life to improve,
for my relationships to feel rich,
and for my mind to finally experience ease
was for me to explore and embrace
the anxious unknown that dwelled within

you can change your location,
meet new people,
and still have the same old problems.

to truly change your life,
you need to look inward,
get to know and love yourself,
and heal the trauma and dense conditioning
in your mind.

this is how you get to the root.
internal changes
have a significant external impact.

i kept getting crushed
by my own expectations

barely present
thinking but not feeling
speaking but not listening
interacting but not noticing

smiling to continue the performance

my heart struggled with gratitude

never feeling satisfied
always missing what was in front of me

because my mind kept jumping
into imagining what more i could want

which made everything i was given
never quite as special as what i had envisioned

(disconnected)

after the trauma
i shifted into survival mode

unknowingly, i shielded my being with numbness

numb to letting others in
numb to my inner turmoil
numb to accepting what happened

unknowingly, i fell into a cycle of craving

craving safety
craving nourishment
craving no more pain

my reactions were large and loud
anything that did not go my way
was perceived as a potential threat

my focus centered on protecting
my delicate sense of self
i had little energy to place myself
in anyone else's shoes

it took the constant feeling
of dissatisfaction
and the exhaustion of never feeling
at ease
for me to start pulling myself out of my
dissociated way of living
and finally say "enough" to
a constant state of defense

(before awareness)

the friction
inside your mind
will keep overflowing
into your relationships

until you process
your emotional history
and understand how it shapes
your ego, perception, and reactions

do what is right for you.
do it over and over again.
lean into the light.

keep going even when it is hard.
especially when it is hard.

do not let doubt stop you.
trust the process when your mood is low.

let growth be your mission.
let healing be your reward.
let freedom be your goal.

everyone can benefit from self-healing;
even those who have not
experienced serious trauma
have at one point or another
felt the sting of heavy emotions

the mind feels these moments sharply
and they tend to ripple outward
impacting how we think, feel, and act

though we may learn to cope with mental tension
and the unexpected changes that cause turmoil

by taking a deeper look inward
we may be able to mend old hurt
and release old pain

by taking a deeper look inward
we may gain the courage to *evolve*

into greater mental clarity
into greater happiness
into greater patience
into greater honesty
into greater love

essentials to remember on tough days:

practice patience
accept what you feel
do not punish yourself
make sure you get good rest
give yourself ample kindness
accomplish smaller goals that day
do things that will calm your mind
a bad moment does not equal a bad life
struggle can be a space for deep growth
this current discomfort is not permanent

before you can see
someone else clearly
you must first be aware
that your mind will impulsively
filter what it sees through the lens
of your past conditioning and
present emotional state

sometimes you walk willingly into heartbreak
because it is clear that your time as partners
has run its course. for a while you fit together
seamlessly, but over time your paths have
started to diverge. it has become too hard to
meet each other in the middle and your heart
no longer feels at home. there is only so much
trying you can do before you say enough and
take a new direction. even though the future is
unclear, you know that moving forward alone
is what you need to grow and be free.

taking a moment
to figure out
how you really feel
instead of letting
old patterns decide for you
is one of the most
authentic things you can do

i have built a home with another person a few
times now, always expecting it to be a lasting
haven. as the storms came and went, the homes
would show their weakness and eventually come
apart. being left with the dread of sadness and
the hollow feeling of unwanted new beginnings,
it has finally dawned on me that if i build a
home within myself, a palace of peace created
with my own awareness and love, this can be the
refuge i have always been seeking.

sometimes a person ends a good relationship
because the areas they think are bad are being
intensified by their personal issues that they
have not dealt with properly. sometimes
people break apart a home because they
are unaware of their projections and are
not ready to appreciate a good thing.

heal yourself,
not just so you can thrive,
but to ensure that people
who cross your path in the future
are safer from harm

it is not easy, but the idea is simple:

the more we heal our own wounds, the less
likely we will be to cause intentional or
unintentional harm. perfection is not possible on
the interpersonal level. our individual perceptions
and changing emotions will occasionally cause
misunderstanding and accidental pain, but if we
can show up for each other compassionately, then
we can remedy the hurt that needs tending.

we often hand our tension over to others without
understanding that it wasn't ours to begin with.
someone passed it to us, and so we pass it to the
next person, and they to the next, until it lands in
the hands of someone with the tools to process it
and let it go. the more of us who are open to inner
work, the more points there will be in the giant web
of humanity where harm will not be able to spread.

the self-awareness needed to stop causing ourselves
and others harm is not just about knowing our own
inner mechanics, our trauma, the moments when
we are projecting, or how our reactions impact
our perceptions. it is also about taking the time to
understand what society has encoded in our minds
without our explicit permission.

radical honesty with ourselves is the starting point. it can help us overcome many complexes and help us see that there is much room for improvement. but to get to the root of the matter, to go even deeper, especially into the subconscious where many of our old patterns lie in wait, we need to find a practice that can help us process and unload this conditioning. we do not need to reinvent the wheel. there are already many proven practices that have helped thousands of people take real steps forward in their lives. our task is simply to search and find what works for us and then to commit to the inner journey.

when healing gets deep
there is sometimes
an explosion of emotion
that occurs to clear out
old energetic debris

you feel most agitated
right before you settle
into a more substantial peace

people are incredibly similar and different at the same time. we all have the same basic structure of mind and emotions, but we have distinct mental conditioning because no two people have experienced the same exact life. the twists and turns, the reactions we have felt, the things we have understood and misunderstood, all that we have come to believe, how we perceive ourselves and the world, the maze of patterns that impact our behavior, the different magnitudes of trauma — you can go on and on and see that each individual has their own inner world and unique emotional history.

since we are all so different, what helps one person heal may not help another person. what may seem too hard or too easy for some people may be a good fit for someone else or may be the right fit later on in life. fortunately, we live in a time when healing tools and practices are becoming more accessible. if we try, we can find something out there that meets our conditioning where it is at, something that we find challenging but not overwhelming, something that connects with our intuition, something that we are willing to spend time learning and practicing. there are so many options out there, from many different forms of meditation to a wide variety of therapy practices and many other healing modalities.

it is not about faking calm when

you actually feel turbulent emotions;
it is about accepting what has come up
without adding more tension to it

it is easier to trust people who recognize
when they have made a mistake
and are not afraid to apologize

this is a sign that they have
enough humility to be open to growth

a fresh start begins with forgiveness
and trust is greatly deepened when
changed behavior becomes consistent

neither of us knew
how to handle conflict
without making it worse

we never wanted to argue,
but it kept happening
because that is what hearts do
when they are overflowing with old pain

we did not mean the things we said;
they were just a reflection of the fire
that escalates when two imperfect people
compete to win

how many relationships would have
gone a different way if the goal were
not just to find harmony as a couple,
but to also find harmony
as individuals?

sometimes we wonder why it is taking so long to
change and heal ourselves and why the same sort
of heavy emotions keep coming up. we do not
realize how rapidly we have accumulated patterns
throughout our lives, especially during moments
of intense emotion. after years of repeating the
same behaviors, it takes time to change and adopt
new responses to life. how many times have we
felt anger, sadness, frustration, anxiety, and more?
when we remember this cycle of repetition, it helps
support our patience as we continue the process of
letting go of the old, literally releasing remnants of
the past during moments of deep healing.

one of the most important qualities
to develop in life is determination.

at some point you just have to
put your foot down and say,

"i am going to move in this
new direction and no person
or situation is going to stop me."

great transformations need a beginning.

a real conversation
free from projection
and ego-flexing
is a special gift

most do not talk to listen;
they talk to be heard

self-awareness, selflessness,
and a real desire to listen
are required for mutually authentic
and honest exchange

miscommunication and conflict occur because we are not building a bridge of understanding. often, in heated conversations, all we can think about is our own perspective, emotions, or ego. this limits our ability to empathize with the experience of another person, which is a prerequisite for the harmony that comes from understanding. one of the greatest gifts we can give each other is *selfless listening*, which is hearing someone's truth without projecting one's own emotion or story onto it—literally receiving another's perspective with complete acceptance.

in special moments, we can take turns deeply seeing one another. here we move beyond having an exchange into *holding space* while someone reveals their truth. this is a higher level of listening that involves acting as a compassionate audience for another person without interrupting or adding our own perspective. when we hold space for one another, hearts become more open, truth is ready to be revealed, and old tension comes to the surface so that it can be seen and held, not just by the speaker, but also the listener. this collective honoring of each other's truth can be incredibly healing.

i trust and feel at home around the ones who
are not afraid to be vulnerable with themselves,
who live confidently in their power and gentleness,
who try their best to live without harming others,
who are serious about their growth and healing,
and who have the humility to say, "i do not know."

it is okay to not have the answer

one of the bravest things
you can do
is boldly embrace the unknown,
accept your fear,
and continue to move forward

a clear mission
does not always have a clear path

how many times
has your mind
taken a small piece
of uncertain information
and spun a story around it that
ends up consuming your thoughts?

the mind is inclined to protect itself, but an attitude
of defensiveness easily breeds anxiety. out of
caution, we fixate on uncertain information and
create stories that can lead to unnecessary fear and
mental tension. taking a moment to notice when we
are jumping to conclusions can save us from worry
and grief.

through self-awareness, we can begin to notice
when we are overthinking. the simple act of
bringing our awareness out of the mental clutter
of unreliable thoughts and back into the present
moment can preserve our energy and decrease the
friction we feel.

to be clear, there is nothing wrong with protecting
oneself, but it is helpful to observe how often
we take a defensive stance. if we are only ever
defensive, we are surely getting in the way of our
inner peace.

too many of us project our old conditioning
onto new situations. reactions happen
quickly and are based on past perceptions;
they make it challenging to process what
is happening in an unbiased and objective
manner. if you want to see things clearly,
use your self-awareness to intentionally set
the past aside and take in a fresh perspective.
redirecting your attention preserves your energy.

self-awareness is noticing
the rhythm of your thoughts

feeling when they are clear
and when they are out of sync

knowing when to take them seriously
and when to let them go

not every thought is valuable;
most are just the sounds of
impulsive emotional reactions

real maturity is observing your own
inner turbulence and pausing before
you project how you feel onto
what is happening around you

when you dislike what someone has done
and are quietly rolling in animosity toward
them, you are not only weighing yourself down;
you are strengthening future reactions of anger.
progress is realizing that fixating on what
happened cannot change the past, but a
calm mind can certainly help your future.

sometimes you need to move slowly
so you can then move powerfully

the modern world is so fast paced
that you feel the pressure to keep up

setting aside what everyone else is
doing and moving at your natural speed
will help you make better decisions
and lift up your inner peace

ask yourself:

is this how i actually feel, or
is this my emotional history
trying to recreate the past?

as our self-awareness deepens, we begin to understand that much of who we are and how we see the world is formed through the accumulation of past emotional reactions. these moments of intense feeling leave their mark on the subconscious and predispose us to repeating certain behaviors.

the rapid movements of the mind are so subtle that we can feel as though we are the makers of our present destiny. in reality, the past is constantly pushing itself into the present, inclining us toward replicating old emotions and thoughts. the insistence of our mental past gives us little room to decide for ourselves how we actually want to feel. the past does not take into account how things truly are.

the same way patterns accumulate, they can be released. letting go is possible, but it requires courage, effort, an effective healing technique, and consistent practice. the mind is immensely vast; it takes time to unbind old patterns that recreate the past. when we begin to develop self-awareness and a calm mind, the stories and patterns embedded in our subconscious begin to surface for release.

when we travel inward, we may hit a particularly
rocky layer of the mind, a sediment of conditioning
that has been thickly reinforced. when we let go of
the hardened inner layers, we often feel the impact
of their release in our personal lives: the storms
of yesterday or the heaviness of past moments
rise to the surface. we may feel as though we're
on the edge of turbulence and disharmony as we
open ourselves up to deconditioning. real growth is
recognizing these moments and treating ourselves
gently as the storms pass.

to see your hidden patterns, you need to
intentionally build self-awareness. question
your perception, build a compassionate and
honest internal dialogue, dig deeper into
what your real motivations are, and have
the humility to know you can learn more.
self-awareness combined with action
opens the door to real change.

wisdom is accepting that there
are things you cannot force:

people change when they are ready

creativity moves at its own rhythm

healing does not have a time limit

love blooms when things align

unbinding

time does not heal all wounds; it just gives
them space to sink into the subconscious,
where they will continue to impact your emotions
and behavior. what heals is going inward,
loving yourself, accepting yourself, listening
to your needs, addressing your attachments
and emotional history, learning how to let go,
and following your intuition.

it sometimes feels as though time has helped us heal, but all it has really done is teach us to live with the wound. just because we have stopped thinking about the harm of the past does not mean it is fully healed. the passing of time allows what was first on a conscious level to sink deeper into the mind where it becomes a quiet yet powerful lever that forces us to behave a certain way. underneath our conscious thoughts remains the impact of a harmful yesterday.

healing requires moving inward with patience, honesty, and courage. if we do not address our accumulated subconscious patterns, they will simply remain there, always affecting how we think, speak, and act. our accumulated wounds and conditioning will restrict our flexibility and cause us to get stuck in a loop that continues repeating the past.

heartbreak is not always a sad ending;
sometimes it sets in motion a profound
transformation. it can open the door to truly
loving yourself, becoming more emotionally
mature, and learning what type of partner
would actually support your happiness.

letting go does not mean you have given
up, and it does not mean you no longer care.
it just means that you are releasing the
attachments of the past that get in
the way of your happiness and mental clarity.
letting go is the unbinding and disentangling
of old behavior patterns that pull you
into unnecessary mental tension and worry.
when you can be okay with things not having
gone a certain way, life begins again. making
peace with the past opens you up to love and
adventure and allows you to apply the lessons
you have learned with a new calmness.

many of us do not realize
how much we are actually suffering
until our awareness starts to expand

we do not see that our happiness has a ceiling
created by the sorrows and traumas
we have repeatedly suppressed

we do not realize that our reactions to life's
difficulties
stop us from seeing things clearly and place limits
on our ability to produce more creative solutions

we do not understand how powerfully our
past grips our present

so much of our internal struggle comes from not embracing change. tension decreases when we understand that change is happening at every level, from the atomic, to the biological, to the mental. a human being is composed of moving parts. our identity is no different. it is a dynamic phenomenon, similar to a river—flowing, moving, expanding, roaring, weaving, all the time with power and all the time with the potential to change. do not limit yourself to a static understanding of who you are. release your conditioned boundaries and be free.

may all of the times that someone
has made an incorrect assumption
about you activate a new sense of
humility and patience in your mind
that stops you from doing the same
thing to another person in the future

ask yourself:

is the connection real if there
is no space to be vulnerable?

the depth of our relationships is defined by
how freely we feel we can deliver our authentic
message. the deepest bonds are held together
by a bridge of honesty. real love holds space for
vulnerability, a place where we can be open, raw,
and even share parts of ourselves that are not fully
formed but are ready to be expressed.

whether within ourselves or in front of someone
who is close to us, vulnerability asks for non-
judgmental acceptance of our imperfections. this is
a form of compassion that can help us observe our
story in a different light, hopefully transforming
what was once burdensome into a more insightful
understanding. this is also a form of compassion
that allows us to accept the way things are without
trying to change it. sometimes vulnerability just
asks to be seen and heard.

if we are far away from ourselves, if we are
not honest with ourselves, and if we are full of
unexamined emotions and conditioning, we will
naturally find it difficult to be close to others. it
becomes easier to give loving support when we
have taken the time to explore our own inner world
and let go of the subconscious patterns that do not
align with how we want to show up for one another.

have you noticed that when
you feel the urge to change
someone, what you really want is
for them to behave more like you?

you cannot build a deep connection with someone
who is disconnected from themselves.

when we are in the habit of ignoring what we
feel or consistently run away from hard parts of
ourselves, distance is created not just between
us and ourselves but also between us and other
people. our lack of a full embrace of all that we are
can make our interactions with others superficial.
even if there is a desire to connect deeply with
someone, that connection will encounter limits
and will only ever reach a depth equal to the
relationship we have with ourselves. our personal
degree of self-awareness will reflect dimly or
brightly on whomever crosses our path.

if we can observe our emotions with open arms full
of compassion, it will be much easier to show up
and support others when they are going through a
moment of personal turbulence. if we can embrace
our own complexity, we will have patience as we
learn more about those closest to us. if we have
experience facing our own hard truths and being
present through our personal ups and downs, we
will have the emotional fortitude to wisely handle
challenging moments in a relationship without
immediately running away.

there is no other way to a life of fulfillment, happiness, and vibrant connections, but through thoroughly traveling the realms of our own heart and mind. areas that remain undiscovered are areas of potential friction that may manifest in our own mind or between us and the ones we love. all that is unexplored can show up as blocks that can stop the flow of harmony.

if we are accustomed to brave observation and practicing acceptance when inner turbulence tries to bring our attention to an unexplored or unloved part of ourselves, then the moments of friction within us or in our relationships will not become blocks. instead, these tough moments will become fertile ground to deepen our connection and refine our commitments. simply stated, putting the effort into knowing ourselves can only help us know others better. loving ourselves is essential if we want to live a good life.

when you feel agitated because you
think someone you love is not growing
quickly enough, remember that you had
to go slowly before you could make real
progress. managing your expectations and
knowing that people grow at their own speed
will save you from interrupting your peace.

attachment is not:

having desires, goals,
or personal preferences

attachment is:

the mental tension you feel when you do not
get exactly what you crave; it is refusing
to accept change or let go of control

when desire combines with tension, it morphs
into craving. attachment is when you start craving
things to be a certain way. craving is an extreme
form of desire that quickly attaches to different
ways of feeling and the objects/situations/
people that produce these feelings. attachment
is also when you try to place restrictions on the
unexpected and natural movements of reality. it is a
heightened form of the desire for control.

as the buddha put forth in his teaching, craving
itself gives birth to attachment. this dense form of
clinging to what we crave not only causes much
mental struggle, tension, and dissatisfaction, but it
also clouds our ability to objectively observe what
is happening within and around us.

wanting and craving are not the same thing. simply
wanting is a natural pursuit that focuses our energy.
craving occurs when wanting deepens and becomes
filled with tension or stress. the stress worsens when
we do not succeed in getting the thing we crave.

craving is ultimately the source of our mental
struggle and dissatisfaction. even when our
attachments are successful in molding reality,
we still find ourselves dissatisfied because craving
is an endless pit. once the sensation we pursued
has passed, the mind will return to craving more
because craving is what it knows best.

it is important to note that there is a substantial difference between craving and having goals or preferences. it is possible to pursue our aspirations without the stress that comes with craving and attachment. it is good and healthy to pursue our goals, but it serves us best to do so wisely and in a manner that does not make our happiness dependent on future achievements.

we know that something is a preference or a simple desire when we do not have the fate of our happiness connected to its realization. we know it is a preference when things do not happen the way we want them to and we accept this reality without the intensity of pain or hurt; we know something is an attachment when we feel mental tension, pain, and misery when we do not get what we crave.

sometimes the end is sudden
and you are left without closure,
heartbroken and unprepared
for such a sharp change

for a while, you live with a mind
that is half here and half full of regret,
wondering, "what if?"

for a while, your heart only feels grief
and your mind only sees gray

and then life starts to call you back
into its arena of possibility;
it reminds you that all is not lost
and that even though a chapter ended,
there is still a longer story to be told

with time and intention,
wounds lose their heaviness,
healing fills the tough parts of your being,
and you awaken the light of love within yourself

in time, you will return fully into the precious now
with a heart that feels refreshed and ready to move
forward

how many times has everything
come crashing down and left you feeling
as though the world was over?

now,
how many times
after grieving

have you gotten back up,
embraced the power of your determination,
and moved forward into a new life?

old patterns do not give up easily. they will try
to keep pulling you into reactions that lead into
repeating the past. but in time, after not feeding
them for a while and continually practicing your
ability to pause and respond, they weaken and
become easier to let go. they may still appear as
an option occasionally but will not have the same
strength as before. this is the turning point, the
shift that changes everything, the leap forward you
have been waiting for, the victory when it becomes
clear that you have moved beyond the past and
into a new life where you have matured enough to
intentionally be your own person.

learning how to breathe
and be okay
when my mind
feels dark and gray

to accept
this passing moment
without suppression
or lasting fear

to know that
the clouds moving through me
do not define who i am
or who i will be

learning the art of letting go
has been the skill my mind
has always sought

now i see that i am a river
always changing
while moving gently
in the direction of total liberty

they asked her,

"what is real happiness?"

she answered,

"happiness is not fulfilling every pleasure or
getting every outcome you desire. happiness
is being able to enjoy life with a peaceful mind
that is not constantly craving more. it is the
inner peace that comes with embracing change."

(being)

we often desire change in our lives, yet we reject
the changes that come about spontaneously. this
is a recipe that will repeatedly serve us misery. a
mind full of attachments craves the fulfillment of
its yearning and attempts to mold the world into the
shape it desires.

when we are controlled by our attachments, we
not only lose our peace of mind; we miss the
opportunity to enjoy life's natural unfolding. in
fact, all of the things we love and appreciate exist
because of continuous change. without change, life
itself would not be possible.

real happiness arises when we can love ourselves
and the world while welcoming and appreciating
change. this does not mean that we should live like
rocks and allow the river of change to flow around
us. love naturally motivates us to attempt to mold
the world in a way that enhances love, but wisdom
also teaches that we should not get attached to
things existing in an exact way, because change
will always come.

being okay with not being okay
does not make things
automatically better,

but it does stop you
from adding more tension
to an already difficult situation

being okay with not being okay
helps you let go

tough feelings and agitated thoughts cannot take
over your life when you meet them with ease,
acceptance, and a calm mind. sometimes these
old imprints bring with them visceral, rough
feelings that have been locked away but suddenly
have the space they need to momentarily arise
and evaporate. an important part of letting go is
feeling without reinforcing—you can be honest
with yourself about the heavy emotions that come
up and choose not to act them out or make them
worse. if you meet the rough parts of yourself with
gentleness, they will melt away, leaving you lighter
and giving you more space to act from a place of
wisdom. all you need to do is be okay with not
being okay during tense moments of release.

throw away the idea that you need to
pause your life until you are fully healed;
this is a different way of being attached
to perfection. progress happens when you
make better decisions in the midst of living.
you can simultaneously heal your past
while being open to the present.

.

how many times have you been
unable to fully enjoy a special
moment because you couldn't stop
thinking about what was missing?

when you are in an unavoidable situation
that is frustrating, treat your mental energy
like a precious resource. instead of fueling
your frustration with more agitation, which
will only make your mind more cluttered
and tired, realize that change will
eventually wipe all of this away.

many of our emotional reactions do not
have to do with what is currently going on.
they are actually old emotions accumulated
from the past—patterns that arise when
familiar situations appear.

the mind attempts to see the world in a way that affirms its conditioning. our perception takes in the present by categorizing and understanding what is happening through its similarity to the past—this creates a system of repetition that strengthens old patterns. new events are normally not perceived in their full clarity because their similarity to past situations triggers old emotional reactions, which quickly cloud the mind's ability to observe what is happening objectively. we are seeing today and simultaneously feeling all of our yesterdays.

when trauma becomes a part of your identity,
it is harder to heal. the narratives that define
how you see yourself need space to change.
acknowledging your past is important, but so
is doing the work to unbind those old patterns
so you can move beyond them. allowing your
sense of self to be fluid will support your
happiness. change is always happening,
especially within you.

expectations cause great misery for the individual.
we are constantly creating narratives of how
we want things to be and how we want others
around us to act. these narratives invariably
lead to disappointment because the stories we
crave are often dashed and broken by unrealistic
expectations, circumstances beyond our control,
and the randomness of the external world.

we forget that what unites all human beings is our
ignorance and room for improvement. we each
carry conditioning that clouds our perspective. our
time on earth is an opportunity to overcome mental
limitations such as unforgiving expectations and
a desire to control everything—limitations that
impede us from complete freedom and happiness.

as we do the work of examining our inner world,
it is unfair for others to expect us to be perfect and
for us to expect others to be perfect, especially
when "perfect" often means having others fulfill
our every desire. in a world full of imperfect
people, patience and forgiveness become essential.

it is easier to let go
of someone's opinion of you

when you understand
that others see you through
a combination of their past conditioning
and their current emotional state

without realizing it,
they see themselves first,
and through that lens they get
an unclear picture of you

there may be times when you
feel like a lot of what you've understood
no longer makes sense.

this might make you feel as though
you have regressed, but it is actually
a sign that you are opening new space for
deeper wisdom and greater perception.

when your previous understandings disintegrate,
they are not always immediately replaced by better
or deeper understandings. when you take your
growth seriously, you will often find yourself in
this in-between state;
it is okay to live without clear answers.

growth is not about forcing understanding;
it is about allowing it
to grow organically.

(shedding and expansion)

as you shed old programming and
your perspective expands, what you once
enjoyed may shift and situations that once
caused tension may no longer trouble you.
as your mind becomes clearer and lighter, the
world begins to look new. periods of integration,
in which you get to know yourself again, are
just as important as great leaps forward.

the world is a giant pool of moving vibrations,
waves of energy emitted from all beings.
when we cultivate our minds,
we cleanse our personal vibe.
we reclaim our power by
not yielding to what flows around us
and by allowing what is within us to come forward.
remember, the energy you most often repeat
is the energy you will most easily connect with.
your vibration is always shining
and affecting your environment.

reclaiming your power
is noticing when a story
based on assumptions
is making your mind tense
and intentionally bringing yourself back
to the present moment
as a way to cut the delusion

it is not about managing your
emotions; it is about managing
your reactions to your emotions

our reactions tell us what our mind has internalized from our past experiences. they are dense patterns that rise from the deep subconscious to protect us. this form of defense is not based on wisdom but on survival. when we start expanding our self-awareness, we begin to see that in moments of turbulence we have more effective options than repeating blind behaviors, which produce limited results that generally wipe away our clarity and inner peace.

we are not trying to control or manage the way we feel. we are trying to accept the shifts in our mood as the mind weaves through the large spectrum of emotions, moving from one emotion to the next, spending more time in some than others, but still traveling the whole human experience.

we immediately and unconsciously react to strong emotions. our reactions not only strengthen the emotion we are feeling; they imprint upon and accumulate within the subconscious, priming us to react similarly in the future.

we can manage our reactions, not by controlling
what we feel, but by bringing awareness into the
process. it is hard to change if you cannot see
yourself. the light of awareness is especially useful
when our reaction to a momentary emotion starts to
undo our balance and mental clarity. our awareness
lights up the darkness and helps us to see more
options and information.

when we remember that emotions are
impermanent just like everything else in this
universe, it becomes easier for us to stand next
to the river that is the human mind and watch as
things flow by. self-awareness helps us overcome
blind reactions that make already difficult
situations more turbulent. without self-awareness,
it is difficult to make choices that differ from those
you have made in the past.

your initial reaction is usually your past
trying to impose itself on your present

know your sources of rejuvenation:

the amount of solitude you need to feel fresh again

the activities that strengthen your creativity

the people who light up your spirit

the love
between us

three thoughts:

relationships normally start with two people
wanting to treat each other well. harm is caused
when someone does not know how to properly
manage their reactions to their emotions. if you
think you *are* your emotions, then your words and
actions will resemble your mental turbulence.

in relationships, it is important to understand
that the other person cannot fix your emotional
problems. at best they can support you as you
uncover and process your own emotional history.

there is no such thing as a perfect relationship, but
there are incredible relationships in which the
mutual connection and support are indescribably
profound.

sometimes it takes your heart breaking
a few times for you to become independent
in important and healthy ways. heartbreak shows
you that your self-worth and wholeness should
not depend on another's words or love.
use the hurt as a map that leads
inward to pursue your healing
and ignite your self-love.

throw away the idea that you have to be fully
healed to be in a loving relationship with a great
partner. we normally come together with many
unresolved issues because healing simply takes
time. the couples who shine with harmony are the
ones who commit to healing and growing together.

vibrant relationships
feel like a sanctuary
where you are safe
to bring your vulnerability
and you are given ample love and care

a home
that equally supports
rest and growth
free from judgment
as you both seek to evolve

a union
void of control
but filled with
mutual understanding

it is easy to cause friction and unintentional harm
in a relationship when you do not know yourself
and have spent little time addressing your past
pain. how many relationships have folded under the
weight of unprocessed trauma, unhealthy patterns,
and unchecked reactions?

one of the toughest things
about relationships in which both partners
are open to inner growth
is when your partner uncovers
a thick layer of old conditioning or trauma
that they have to work through

you see them struggle and face the storm
but you cannot fix it for them

all you can do is hold space and
be ready to give them loving support

attributes of a good relationship:

selfless listening
calm communication
holding space for each other
strong trust, no need to control
authenticity, no need to perform
rest, laughter, and adventure together
the love between you is empowering
commitments to each other are clear
flexible, no need to always be together
both have the space to grow and change

attributes of a good friend:

they feel like home
they are honest with you
they remind you of your power
they support you in your healing
they have a revitalizing presence
they hold a vision of your success
they support you in new adventures
they lift you up with joy and laughter
they bring out the best version of you

friendships that feel like home are naturally disarming. they remind us that we can stop the performance and come forward the way we authentically feel. the deepest bonds are spaces where vulnerability is welcome. good friendships have a reciprocal quality. when either person is experiencing struggle, the other is ready to hold space, to listen without judgment and with a heart full of compassion. meaningful friendships contain a bond that rises above competition. we feel a friend's victory as if it were our own. true sympathetic joy—the joy we feel for the success of another—is the absence of jealousy.

friends who feel like family are rare.
when you are together, a timeless spark
lights up the path to joy, shared learning,
and rejuvenation. you seek to support
each other's happiness and naturally
rejoice in each other's success.

throw away the idea that you need to
find a perfect partner or a flawless friend.
all people are imperfect. what is possible
is connecting with someone who is doing
their own inner work. they will have more
practice with authenticity, holding space,
intentional growth, and self-awareness.

honesty
+
natural bond
+
laughter and joy
+
genuine mutual support
+
revitalizing interactions
+
authentic communication

=

empowering friendships

some of the biggest tests in life come when tough things happen in your closest circle, when family or friends who hold a piece of your heart go through a struggle that you have no control over, when all you can do is rise to the occasion by listening to their words and radiating the love you feel for them. though it is not for you to decide how things will turn out, you can support, provide comfort, and remind them that your love for them is real and will remain unbroken.

some relationships do not have harmonious
beginnings. there is an undeniable pull that
brings the two together, but there is also
a distance between them created by their
unhealed hearts. this space within them,
filled with the unknown and unseen, causes
miscommunication between the two, friction,
and sometimes even unintentional pain. how
can they treat each other well when they
are still mysteries to themselves? the shift
comes when both commit to turning inward
to heal and know themselves. naturally, this
brings them closer together and elevates
the love and support they share.

conflict worsens when two people
fall into defensive reactions. then there
is no real communication happening,
only trauma arguing with trauma.

for real communication to happen, all projections
need to cease. two people cannot see each other
clearly and find common ground if both are
thinking and speaking through dense clouds of
emotion. so many relationships and friendships
break because we do not have the tools and
emotional maturity to see beyond our defensive
reactions. when we notice our own defensiveness,
pause, and come into a clearer thinking space, we
have the opportunity for real conflict resolution.
without vulnerability, patience, and self-awareness
on both sides, there cannot be reconciliation.

without listening, honesty, and space for safe
vulnerability, there is no communication. when we
intentionally elevate the level of communication,
the focus switches from telling someone how we
believe they are, to clearly explaining our own
perspective and how we feel. we can certainly
share ways to better support each other, but first we
need to accept each other's truth and move on from
there. the support we ask for cannot be coercive;
our partner needs to voluntarily commit to it for the
union to be healthy.

blind loyalty does not nourish anyone

supporting those you love in their ignorance,
or even worse, continuously tolerating the harm
they cause you, is a serious act of self-betrayal

when you see your loved ones doing
wrong or walking into deeper darkness,
do not follow just because of
an old bond you may share

you do not need to sink together
you do not need to burn together
you do not need to crash together

even though it may be hard,
sometimes you have to listen to
your deepest sense of well-being
and go your own way to
preserve the good inside of you

maturity in a relationship is not expecting to always be on the same schedule. you are not always going to feel good at the same time. one may need more rest than the other, one may need more time to heal, one may pick up new habits more easily. people naturally grow, learn, and move at different speeds.

they asked her,

"what makes a relationship flourish?"

she answered,

"two people who seek to know, love, and heal
themselves as individuals will have harmony flow
between them as a couple. control creates tension,
but trust leaves space for individuality and opens
the door to vulnerability. calm communication,
clear commitments, and the willingness to support
each other's happiness make the union stronger."

(a vibrant partnership)

love is rejuvenated
when partners
occasionally ask each other,

"how can i better
support your happiness?"

a partner who supports your power is priceless;
someone who appreciates your opinions, who
has faith in your dreams and knows that you can
achieve great things. they recognize that you are
whole as an individual but are ready to complement
your life with their love and dedication. together,
you share the responsibility of leadership. with
gentle honesty and open communication, you
check in often to make sure you understand
each other well and are doing what you
can to strengthen your union.

a healthy relationship
is when two people equally take turns
being the one who steps up
when the other is going through
a turbulent moment

each is capable of listening
and holding space

each is self-aware enough
to check in with themselves
and not project onto the other

find a partner who is not afraid to grow.
if they are ready to notice their patterns,
let go of old conditioning, and expand their
perspective, then they will be ready to support
a vibrant relationship. two people who are
working on knowing and loving themselves
as individuals will naturally deepen their
love and understanding of each other. growth
comes with ups and downs, but it is also the
key to great harmony.

we walk through time together
holding hands
as the world changes
living in love
as we grow as individuals
meeting each other in the middle
as our youth gives way to maturity

loving people
does not mean
you let them hurt you

loving yourself and others
unconditionally
is a balance between
protecting yourself
and giving to others

find a partner who is as committed to
supporting you in good times as they are
in the tough moments of growth and healing.
coming together as imperfect people can be
challenging. imperfection can sometimes cause
unintentional conflict, especially when one is
going through a moment of inner turbulence.
patience, calm communication, and selfless
listening get couples through the storm.
conflict decreases when both turn inward
and focus on building self-awareness.

throw away the idea that your partner
can make you happy. they can be great
support, treat you well, and bring so many
good things into your life, but happiness
is only sustainable when it comes from within.
your perception, healing, growth, and
inner peace are your own to create.

find a partner who can appreciate your complexity.
old conditioning from the past, behavior patterns,
changing emotions, your true goals and guidance
from your intuition—this flowing combination
comes together to create who you are. when you
focus on growing and letting go, there are many
layers to unbind and shed. real love is finding a
new harmony as you both evolve, taking the time
to check in and find a new balance as your likes
and dislikes align with your most recent growth.

real love is not always glamorous;
it is about being there when it counts
like when you have a tough day
and your partner sits quietly next to you
holding your hand
listening closely as you reveal
your worries
your inner struggles
and your brightest dreams

relationships take time to flourish. some people expect profound harmony immediately, but harmony is not possible without deep knowledge of one another's likes, dislikes, emotional history, and goals. the more you learn about each other, the more you refine your rhythm together. communication helps channel the love you feel for one another into clear ways of supporting each other's happiness. perfection is not an option, but you can undoubtedly build a great union in which you both feel safe, understood, and loved.

when an argument starts
your goal should be to arrive
at a mutual understanding

it helps to become aware of the inner tension
that is impacting your reasoning

notice your level of attachment
explain yourself clearly
listen with patience

find the balance between honoring your truth
and reflecting on your partner's perspective

and remember that success
is both of you feeling heard

maturity in a relationship is not expecting your partner to constantly be happy. ups and downs are natural. giving each other space to feel heavy emotions while staying attentive and actively supporting one another is a sign of real love. relationships are not about fixing everything for each other; they are about experiencing joyful moments and tough times as a team and loving each other through the changes. sometimes your partner needs to go through their own process to emerge lighter and freer than before.

how can we have a real conversation if every
time we speak i can see in your eyes that my
words are not reaching you? they stop at a
narrative you have created about me based
on who i was many years ago.

make deep connections, not deep attachments

with proximity comes the possibility for
connection. if we are in close contact with
someone, there is the potential for an intuitive
alignment to flourish. after spending a bit of time
with someone, we may desire to spend more time
with them. or we may simply be crossing paths.

as the connection deepens, so does the desire to
treat each other well. we go from being strangers
to becoming known supporters of each other's
happiness. even within families and friendships,
the bonds we experience are built on connection.
connection is based in the mind's innate ability
to love. however, the mind also contains a strong
drive to crave, which ends up conditioning our
perceptions of what we encounter and our reactions
to what we feel.

the deep connections that we feel toward our loved
ones are often wrapped up and mixed in with
attachments, not because we wish to make things
difficult, but because the mind has a strong tendency
to crave and control. attachments cloud the true love
that deep connections emanate. attachments create
much friction in relationships because they stand in
the way of individual freedom.

there is nothing wrong with wanting certain things
in a relationship, but we must resist coercing
others. instead we should build strong pathways
of honest and calm communication so that both
people can feel clearly understood. it is through
this mutually shared understanding that each
individual commits voluntarily to supporting the
harmony of the relationship.

a love without attachment is not a love without
commitment. attachments are attempts at
control marked by deep inner tension; voluntary
commitments are attempts at supporting happiness
and harmony marked by generosity.

base your relationship on clear communication
and voluntary commitments, not expectations

too often, we keep our expectations to ourselves or we only partially hint at what we want. we do not realize that we would be better off exploring the ways we wish to be supported through clear communication. when we are straightforward with others about what we need to feel safe and loved, we give them the opportunity to show up for us.

we are all different. even when we share a clear connection that we can build on, we still need to learn one another's likes, dislikes, strengths, past emotional struggles, and reactive patterns.

communicating our needs, desires, and personal emotional history gives both people the information they need to better understand each other and the opportunity to feel the natural volition to commit and say, "these are the areas where i can do my best to meet you. this is how i can try my best to show up for you." in this way, we transform our private expectations into opportunities for commitment.

the difference here is subtle but important. there
is much greater harmony in a relationship when
neither party is attempting to be in control of it.
expectations are often attachments to shaping
outcomes, and they may leave one or both
partners feeling cornered and powerless. freedom
amongst people, in relationships and outside of
them, is based on understanding and voluntary
commitments, situations in which no one feels
pushed to be a certain way. when we transform our
expectations into opportunities for commitment,
we are cultivating freedom in our relationships.
even when clear communication and voluntary
commitments are practiced, we should still watch
out for manipulative behavior. the desire for
control can reappear in quiet ways, sometimes even
unconsciously. you know voluntary commitments
are being respected when you can freely say no to
a request without resistance, especially if it feels
outside of the bounds of your personal safety/
comfort/goals. every request will not be met with a
yes, especially when both partners are growing and
changing. in their essence, voluntary commitments
need to be optional.

there is nothing wrong with knowing what your needs are in a relationship, but they are better met when they are clearly communicated and when *they match up with what someone is willing to do for you out of their own desire to support you.* when partners make commitments to each other of their own volition, they create space for harmony to flow abundantly in the relationship.

find a partner who can give you the space
you need to be your own person. it is healthy
to have different interests, likes, and dislikes.
you do not need to become the same person
to prove your love to each other. you know
you are both supporting each other's happiness
when each of you feels like you can be your truest
self. remember, trust blossoms in the absence
of control, and vibrant relationships should feel
like a balance of freedom and home.

your partner should accept you as you are
but also help you feel safe enough
to do the deep work of healing and growth

not because they want to change you
but because their presence energizes
and inspires you to flourish
into greater emotional maturity

it is not about finding perfection in another person;
it is about realizing when you come across
an undeniable connection that nourishes your
being and matches the type of support you are
looking for. getting lost in the idea of perfection
is a hindrance. when two people embrace their
imperfections and commit to growing into better
versions of themselves, they will naturally
experience greater happiness in the relationship.

find a partner who is willing to make clear commitments. you both know that supporting each other's happiness is not a mystery, it is the art of communication combined with action. what you need from each other will change over time. by building a culture of checking in regularly, your union will remain harmonious and vibrant. the way you love, trust, and show compassion for each other elevates your relationship into a space where you can both deepen your personal healing. true love does not fear change, it embraces new growth and adjusts accordingly.

having conversations without assumptions or projections brings a couple closer together. taking turns to really listen, using compassion to reflect on the other person's perspective, intentionally checking in with ourselves during the conversation to see if we are being honest and clear—this makes a difference and builds real harmony. when both partners try to bring a high degree of presence into their interactions with each other, it sets the stage for true love to rise above discord and for understanding to cool the fires of confusion.

it is not about finding a partner who
has flawless emotional maturity; it is
about finding someone who can match
your level of commitment—not just to
the relationship, but commitment to heal
themselves so they can love better, see
more clearly, and have more presence

find a partner you do not have to perform for.
when you are both committed to honesty and have
active compassion for each other, there is no need
to behave in ways that are not genuine. true love
is welcoming each other's changing emotions with
open arms. though you are both dedicated to
becoming the best versions of yourselves, you also
understand that not every day will be a good day
and not every step will be a step forward. being in
a relationship with a high degree of authenticity
and gentleness allows both partners to let down
their guards and feel at home.

the deepest friendships
reveal themselves during moments of crisis

when your world is shaken,
a friend stands and faces the storm with you

when things look dim,
they bring their light to remind you
that better days are coming

when you feel challenged,
they help you see your power

some friendships are so profound
that when you spend time together
it feels as though you have slipped
into another dimension:

a space where you both feel free and safe to
share the realest versions of yourselves,

a home where time stops and joy
shines without limits.

an irreplaceable friend is someone who:

highly values your trust
appreciates your honesty
naturally feels like family
still loves you as you change
finds it easy to laugh with you
holds space for you in tough times
supports your happiness and safety
helps you to believe in your self-worth
inspires you to love and know yourself

real maturity in a relationship is letting
your partner know when your mind feels
heavy before your thoughts find
a way to blame them for your tension;
openly naming that you are experiencing
turbulence allows you to know it is there
and your partner to know that it is time
to support you or hold space.

some friends hold a special place
in your story. they were there when
times were tough, they saw you clearly
when others did not, they believed in
you before you believed in yourself.
bonds that lift you up are precious
and easily go on to last a lifetime.

true love will accept you as you are but also
help you feel comfortable to shed the old and
transform into the greater you. many arrive
into a new relationship half-healed and half-
hurting. a mixture of thriving and surviving.
when the connection is genuine, supportive
of clear commitments, each person can start
to dig deeply into their individual healing, to
unfold and release the layers/stories that are
waiting deep within. progress in personal
healing ultimately elevates the mutual
joy of partnership.

growing

eventually you start to see changes.
your mind becomes light, the trees look
bright, the air you breathe begins to feel
like food for new opportunity, and life
takes on a crisp color pattern. ups and
downs will continue to come and there is
still much to learn, but you are calm now
and do not fear the old storms, which seem
to pass more quickly. a new awareness arises
to gently remind you that your power is
yours to wield and is ready to propel you
forward into peace and liberating insight.

be prepared to meet a new version
of yourself every time you shed another
layer of old trauma, conditioning, or hurt.
as you let go, your perspectives and interests
will shift. transformation is natural as you
travel the road to greater self-awareness,
happiness, and peace.

the goal is not to heal
and then begin your life.
the goal is to embrace healing
as a lifelong journey and allow
genuine connections
to emerge organically
along the way.

feeling emotionally exhausted is common
after opening up deeply or after experiencing
a series of heightened emotions for an extended
period of time. be prepared to take the quiet time
and solitude you need to fully rejuventate.
you are allowed to not be serious all of the time.

real courage is listening to your intuition
even when society and people in your life advise
against it

a lot of advice comes from fear,
people wishing you to stay with the herd
and do the normal thing

taking a calculated risk is not recklessness;
it is fearlessness

do not think in extremes; the answer is
rarely all or nothing. skillful action is finding
pathways even amidst contradictory options.
solutions are found by going beyond the
superficial and into the subtle. understand
that life is the integration of complexity.
everything is situational and multilinear.
find the middle path and challenge
yourself to think deeper.

give love, but don't exhaust yourself
be peaceful, but don't become passive
have patience, but don't settle for less
trust yourself, but don't develop arrogance
be open to love, but don't force a connection
have goals, but don't chase after each craving

when in doubt, remember you have:

the power to say no
the authenticity to be you
the patience to keep learning
the fortitude to continue trying
the courage to embrace change
the fearlessness to give selflessly
the wisdom to cultivate inner peace
the bravery to fulfill your aspirations
the openness that grows friendships
the awareness to follow your intuition
the intelligence to not repeat the past

they asked her,

"what does letting go mean?"

she answered,

"letting go does not mean erasing a memory or
ignoring the past; it is when you are no longer
reacting to the things that used to make you feel
tense and you are releasing the energy attached to
certain thoughts. it takes self-awareness, intentional
action, practice, and time. letting go is the act
of getting to know yourself so deeply that all
delusions fall away."

(presence)

it is not about expecting your partner
to make you happy; it is about clearly
communicating the best ways they
can support you as you travel inward
to ignite your own happiness

it is not possible to erase memories
or change the past, but you can stop
old behavioral patterns, decrease the
intensity of blind reactions, learn to
embrace change, accept all emotions
that come up, build self-awareness,
and strengthen good habits. healing
is intentional action plus time.

it is hard to see your progress
when you are deeply
immersed in the process

before you let doubt
take control

examine how much
you have grown and accomplished
by mentally taking a big step back
so you can look at the whole picture

we feel so safe with the ones we love
that we often share with them
our tension, our stress, our fear,
our sadness,
and even our anger

but let us remember to also
give them the best version of ourselves,
our joy and happiness, our excitement
and peace, our attention and care

gratitude makes you happy
attachment makes you struggle
gentleness reveals inner wisdom
harshness reveals inner turbulence
calmness supports good decisions
solitude supports transformation

essentials for growth:

proper rest
more learning
consistent honesty
building new habits
letting go of old stories
saying no to old patterns
believing that you can change
saying yes to supportive people
examining your emotional history
finding a practice to heal past pain
making time to build self-awareness

so often we spend our time living for tomorrow, eagerly seeking results that can only come with the slow buildup of consistent effort. especially in regard to our own personal transformation, we forget that building new ways of being does not come quickly or with ease. a sturdy temple of peace with a strong foundation that can withstand storms does not appear overnight.

our anticipation of the future gets in the way of our awareness of the present. a mind that is half in the future is partially consumed in a dream—a dream that can only become real through honoring what is in front of us in the here and now.

every breath we take happens in the present. every advancement in our growth happens in the present. the wisdom that comes through feeling the truth of nature can only accumulate within us through our observation of the present. even when we rightfully examine the past or plan for the future, the helpful information we receive and integrate arrives to us in the present.

when we set our goals, we set the stage for growth.
from then on, in the moments that pass, we take
opportunities to align our actions in a way that
steers us in the direction of our aspirations. but if
we do not honor and appreciate every small victory,
if we do not feel gratitude for acting in the way that
supports our transformation, then we will lack the
practice to fully appreciate the accomplishment of
our bigger goals.

remember, always craving specific results is a
form of bondage that not only limits our progress
but reinforces our inability to feel gratitude. the
opposite of craving more is a gratitude that says
"yes" and "thank you" to the present.

you do not need
a partner to feel whole
you do not need
to have everything figured out to feel successful
you do not need
to be fully healed to feel peace
you do not need
to be fully wise to feel happy

embracing yourself as you are
reinforces your worth and
decreases the friction in your mind

embracing ourselves as we are makes moving
forward into a better version of ourselves much
easier. sustainable personal growth requires
balance. if we hate who we are, it will slow the
work down—aversion increases mental friction.
while accepting where we are with radical honesty
can be difficult, as it can be hard to admit our
flaws, even to ourselves, it is the first important
step to real change.

if we can accept our imperfections and understand
that our conditioning limits our perception of
reality, this allows us to more easily begin the work
of undoing the past that is embedded in the mind.
there is a middle path where we can recognize the
characteristics that we want to develop without
adding the tension of aversion to our self-analysis.
embracing ourselves does not mean complacency;
it is the start of a journey into great mental clarity
and love for ourselves and all people.

one of the clearest signs of personal growth is
greater self-love, self-awareness, and love for all
people. inner work is not meant to turn us into
hermits or make us more self-centered. if we are
only reserving our kindness for ourselves, then
something is not right. if we are really trying
to grow our inner peace and wisdom, then our
capacity for empathy and compassion for others
will also grow.

inner work simultaneously makes us stronger
and increases our humility. we reclaim our power
and more easily follow our calling, but we also
recognize how fallible our perceptions can be and
how much more we have to learn.

when we go inward, we realize how much society
has conditioned us, created subtle shifts in our
preferences, and slowly formed our unconscious
biases. we think we are unbiased, but the record
of our past — meaning all interactions we have
experienced and all media we have consumed — is
always impacting our thoughts and actions. real
freedom is the ability to observe the world without
allowing our personal past to impose itself on what
we encounter. at their height, objectivity and selfless
love become one. practice makes a difference.

real friends know you have a range of expressions,
moods, and multiple aspects to your character

they embrace you as you are
and do not want you to perform

they know authenticity is not
being the same person over and over again;
it is allowing yourself to change
as you navigate life

heal at the pace
you know is right for you

what works for someone else
may not be what you need

each person holds
a unique emotional history

discomfort is part of growth,
but constant discomfort
is not healthy

self-love is balancing serious
inner work with rest and ease

slow moments are common
after a period of serious growth

they should not be feared
but embraced as opportunities
to get to know the new you

as you mature, you release so many layers
that you sometimes change radically,
and your mind and body feel like a new home

slow moments are for renewal
and integration of recent lessons learned

but a slow pace often finds a way
to test how you have grown;
this is an important time to observe your progress
and notice where you need further work

inner peace is not:

feeling perfect all of the time or
not caring about what is happening

inner peace is:

feeling and being with your emotions
without reacting to them; it is the calmness
that emerges when you embrace change

six things make inner peace easier:

not being afraid of change

kindness toward others

honesty with yourself

intentional actions

self-awareness

gratitude

life is difficult
and full of unexpected challenges

even so, you have to ask yourself:

how much stress and mental tension
are you unnecessarily causing yourself
by creating assumptions
and replaying fears in your mind?

how often are you refusing to let go
and adapt when things change?

how much of your inner turmoil
is self-imposed?

let's stop treating each other like machines.
it is okay if someone does not immediately
respond to your email. do not expect quick
replies to every text message. the internet
and social media have sharply increased
the demands on your personal energy.
be a human and take your time.

at a time when so many are striving to
get the attention of others, save yourself
the agitation by turning inward and igniting
your own self-worth. social media can be a
vehicle for inspiration or it can intensify your
insecurities. be mindful of how the content
you consume is impacting your emotions.

one of the hardest things about saying
no is potentially upsetting others. if you
know your path and what you need to focus
on, you have to be mindful of your limits.
save your energy so that you can accomplish
the goals at the top of your list. those attuned
to inner work will understand and respect
your right to say no.

for a few days i lost my way
and the past came roaring back

covering my eyes while old impulses
took their chance to reign over my mind

i let myself get caught
in the hurricane of yesterday

sampling my old home
remembering its walls and limits

feeling once again all of the reasons
why i decided to move on

the joy was empty
and what was once fun fell flat

i could not live comfortably in a home
too small for my recent expansion

i felt an immense wave of guilt
for taking a few steps back

but then it hit me
that reexperiencing
these old patterns and ways of being
was the motivation i needed
to finally close the door
and no longer feed the actions
that could only lead me in circles

they asked her,

"what is real freedom?"

she answered,

"freedom is mental clarity combined with inner
peace. freedom is when you can see without
projecting and when you can live without causing
yourself unnecessary mental tension or stress.
it exists whenever you are not craving more.
happiness and freedom are one."

(a clear mind)

check in with yourself occasionally
by asking these three questions:

is this the direction i want to be moving in?

are my recent choices helping my happiness?

what can i change to better support my goals?

practice the strengths of earth

have a giving nature
be grounded in your purpose
hold firm in times of turbulence

cultivate the qualities of water

move through life with gentleness
have access to your power at all times
flexibility and persistence increase success

embody the teachings of fire

transmute what you experience into light
be strong enough to have clear boundaries
have an awareness of when you need more fuel

internalize the values of air

release your expectations
embrace the constant movement of change
seeing is not everything; feeling is essential

(balance)

emotional maturity
is knowing the difference
between your true needs
and temporary cravings

your needs help you live
at an optimal level
and support your happiness

cravings are a reflection
of your agitation and attachments;
they leave you dissatisfied
and wanting more

overcomplicating your healing is something
to watch out for. you do not need to overthink
your past and repeatedly reimagine each trauma.
self-awareness has more to do with the present
moment—if you can see yourself clearly now,
you are more likely to act wisely. The best way
to access and heal your past is by not running
away from yourself in the present moment.

getting unsolicited advice is one of the best tests
and a great time to check in with yourself.

are they saying this for my benefit or their own?

does this advice connect with my intuition?

can i still treat them with patience and compassion
even if their advice felt unnecessary?

one of the hardest skills to master is
saying no to yourself so that you can
rise up and unfold into a greater you:

no to distractions or lack of consistency

no to the patterns and ways of being
that only lead back into the past

no to only doing what is easy

no to doubt and fear

a new life

power is visible in gentle movements

barriers bend and fall when we interact
with each other through an invitation
instead of a push

kindness has a disarming quality

because it carries a warmth that says,

"i am not interested in harming you"

take the risk

choose the direction you feel
burning in your intuition

life is a unique opportunity;
you can make best use of it
when you rise above fear

walking the uncommon path
is not a certain victory,
but it does provide the greatest
possibility for fulfillment

when she started letting go, her vision
became clearer. the present felt more
manageable and the future began to
look open and full of bright possibilities.
as she shed the tense energy of the
past, her power and creativity returned.
with a revitalized excitement, she
focused on building a new life in which
joy and freedom were abundant.

your relationships improve drastically and the
tension in your mind decreases significantly
when you can simply accept people for who
they are instead of fixating on how they
should change in order to be more
like you

six signs of maturity:

being open to vulnerability, learning, and letting go

seeing more perspectives than just your own

accepting responsibility for your happiness

prioritizing practices that help you grow

pausing to think instead of reacting

honesty with yourself and others

cultivate your humility
by questioning your perception
cultivate your humility
by not looking down on others
cultivate your humility
by not making assumptions
cultivate your humility
by being generous often
cultivate your humility
by learning from others

four teachers that give free lessons:

change

water

solitude

being

if i am always wanting
i have little time for being

only in being
can i feel real peace

maturity is feeling joy
for another's success

a mind trapped in competition,
one that feels a quiet bitterness
whenever someone gets a thing you crave,
is a sign that you are still at war with yourself

end the turmoil and friction by loving
and knowing yourself more deeply

even after healing significant trauma
and old conditioning, you will not be happy
all of the time. it is natural for your mood
to go up and down. what does change is
that you react less to old triggers and
when the mind feels turbulent you do
not fall easily into past patterns.

judging yourself by the first impulse
that pops up in your mind is unfair

that is just a copy of who you were in the past

what you intentionally decide to do
shapes who you are and influences who you will be
in the future

remember: pause, think, act

an honest and deep conversation with
a good friend is sometimes the exact
nourishment you need to regain clarity,
get back up, face the world, and resume
your mission with a new and focused energy

three signs of a good friend:

you do not have to perform for them

they hold space for you during struggles

they are truly happy for your success

progress is acknowledging where you are
and where you want to be without allowing
the space between the two to cause you
mental tension. if anything, it should inspire
you to continue moving forward peacefully
and diligently. having goals without attachments
produces faster results.

hurts travel through time

from one person to another
this unwanted heaviness moves
from the past into the present
and then into the future

one of the most heroic things
anyone can do is break the line of hurt

when people heal themselves,
they stop the hurt from multiplying
and their relationships become healthier

when people heal themselves,
they also heal the future

how people perceive you
is more reflective of
their inner mechanics
than your actions

you cannot control
how others think and live,
but you can be intentional
about the energy you put into the world

some may misunderstand you,
but what matters most is that you
understand you

real changes reveal themselves slowly. all this
work of letting go and building self-awareness
gives life a new, fresh feel. when you look out into
the world, you observe a reinvigorated vibrancy
that shines with the opportunity for a better life.
you use the power of choice, even when your
patterns try to pull you in an old direction. you
learn the value of accepting the emotions that come
up and being okay when you are not okay; this
allows moments of turbulence to pass quietly,
leaving your mind lighter and your eyes clearer.
you embrace a life of growth and the truth of
change so that inner peace can become your new
home.

happiness is being able to
enjoy the things you worked for
without slipping into
thinking about what is missing
or what you want next

saying no is a sign of progress
saying no is a sign of commitment
saying no is a sign of empowerment

saying no can help you fulfill your goals
saying no can support your mental health
saying no can bring you to the right people

in a world that is changing
and growing ever more rapidly,
inner calm is your most valuable asset

the type of calm that you can rely on
when there is turmoil around you

the type of calm that helps you
breathe deeply and make good decisions
when it is time for action

calmness helps the mind see clearly

comparison reinforces your anxiety

patience creates space for growth

anger ignites fear-based reactions

joy appears in the present moment

to release a grudge or a story
that is impacting your perception

remember that what you are seeing
is limited and cannot include the full
context of the situation

what you think happened is not final;
there is more to the story

it is not about having light
and kind thoughts all the time;
it is about not feeding the heavy
and mean thoughts. literally letting
them pass without allowing them to
take root and control your actions.

as we move into deeper wisdom, we become
motivated by a growing sense of compassion for
ourselves and others. it is easier to understand
others and what drives their actions when we
understand our own inner world.

as our conscious thinking evolves, we become
gentler with ourselves and others. a new loving
positivity emerges from releasing the tension of
ego and allowing clarity to come forward—the
essence of healing ourselves.

however, this gentleness and positivity should
not be confused with a complete transformation.
we can see signs of a new clarity emerging, but
we must remember that the mind is vast, and the
subconscious, where most of our emotional history
is stored, holds much that still needs to be released.
we are in a situation where our conscious thought
patterns may have changed for the better, but our
subconscious thoughts, the ones that sometimes
spontaneously emerge, are still filled with the
heaviness and harshness of old ways.

this is not to say that we should force ourselves to
think a certain way or push down certain thoughts.
we should just be aware that this lack of a linear
trajectory is a natural part of the healing process
and instead focus on cultivating the habits and
practices that are helping us transform.

the thing about opening yourself up to healing
and growth is that, once some issues melt away,
deeper layers will have the space they need to
come up for observation and release. there is much
more accumulated in the subconscious than we
can initially comprehend. this is why letting go
is a long-term commitment. it is possible to get
to a much happier place while still working on
processing and undoing old patterns.

a strong self-love
helps you find a balance
between giving selflessly
and protecting yourself from harm

finding ourselves can lead to confusion
because who we are is always changing

finding ourselves can be complicated
without any deep healing

it is to our greater benefit to focus our efforts
on *freeing ourselves* from the burden of past pain
and patterns that do not serve our happiness

as we purify our being,
as we release the heaviness that dwells within,
everything about ourselves
and what we should do with our time becomes
clearer

our deepest aspirations become evident
the more we remove the dense clouds of ego
that wrap themselves around our consciousness

attachments are experts
at hiding in plain sight;
the mind may think it sees clearly
but its perceptions are often skewed.

only in the absence of ego
is there objective observation.
as "i" decreases,
wisdom is given space to be.

when you create something,
do not watch its progress
with attachment and anxiety

create it and let it go

give it to the world and let it be

feeling stressed over the outcome
and radiating vibrations of agitation
does not help you or your work

you know from your own growth
that real change is possible

even those who have caused much harm
contain this same dynamic potential

some may change more quickly than others
but the truth remains the same

with the right inner motivation
anyone can become
a better version of themselves

the future you will thank you for listening
to your intuition, for upholding boundaries that
supported your inner thriving, for saying no to
things that did not align with your values, for
taking the time to build your self-awareness,
and for staying true to your vision.

it is important
to understand yourself

but most of healing
is not an intellectual process

it is more about feeling
without trying to avoid

how we act is greatly impacted by the
subconscious patterns that control our
perception of reality

how we feel is deeply affected by our past
emotional history—heavy emotions that do their
best to recreate themselves in the present

what we see can only become objective
and clear when we observe, accept, and let go
of what was silently waiting deep within us

when we rise above the past and use our effort
to respond to life intentionally, by having the
perseverance to build wiser habits, we open
the door wider to living in a new way

the emotional discomfort we feel when we open
ourselves up to letting go is not always directly
connected to a particular tough or traumatic event.
much of our conditioning is generated in seemingly
small, everyday moments. reactions of jealousy,
anger, doubt, and low self-worth are easily
forgotten by the conscious mind, but they
can accumulate in the subconscious in a
way that primes us to feel them again.

in an era of uncertainty and unpredictability,
these qualities will make life easier:

a strong determination
a willingness to keep growing
the patience to listen to your intuition
the ability to adapt to unexpected changes
knowledge of what strengthens your inner peace
knowledge of your values and
the ability to stick to them

a successful life is created
with two words: "yes" and "no"

have the courage to say "yes"
only when it feels right

and "no" to the old patterns
that do not serve you

while your intentional actions
start to change
and your authentic feelings
begin to shift

your thoughts may need
some time to catch up with you

focus on being the more mature, more patient
"you" and old patterns will lose their strength

your thoughts will eventually align
becoming gentler and truer

•

do not expect perfection from yourself
even if you have done a great amount of
internal work

progress is acting intentionally
more often than you act blindly

and not punishing yourself
because you still have room to grow

allow mistakes to peacefully inform
your growth and learning process

you can tell humanity is maturing
because more of us are saying no to harm

we are taking time
to examine our biases,
moving our love from
being selective to unconditional
and expanding our idea
of what is possible

more of us are healing ourselves
and actively helping heal the world

in many ways, a human being is a microcosm of
the world. the conditioning that has accumulated
over time within the mind parallels the systems
that have become dominant within human society.
the reactive patterns of behavior that have been
repeated and reinforced throughout our lives as
individuals mirror the rigidity and slow change of
society at-large.

our minds are, in large part, the way they are
because of the countless defensive reactions we
have knowingly and unknowingly repeated. like
our minds, our world suffers from this pattern.
historically, people in positions of power have
tended to act blindly, allowing past fear and
trauma to inform their present.

as those who have delved into inner work know,
it takes time and self-awareness to break from
the past. it takes the repetition of positive and
nurturing behaviors that work against the flow of
ignorance and fear. more than anything, it takes
intentional action that arises from self-awareness
to break old habits that keep us from thriving. this
process happens at the collective level too. people
must think and feel together before they move
into action against systems of harm.

the importance of self-love and self-acceptance
in personal transformation work is critical. this
is the energy that allows us to embrace ourselves
completely and move forward with less friction
into healthier ways of living. similarly, humanity is
currently experiencing an expansion of compassion.
more individuals are recognizing that their love had
limits and are working to expand it to include all
people.

before healing takes place, the primary motivators
of most human beings are craving and aversion. the
accumulation of craving and aversion throughout
history has formed the society we know today. all of
this is held under a system of short-sighted, greed-
based economics that threatens our ability to live
well on our planet. collectively, we have not yet
learned how to accept our differences and treat them
without fear, nor have we stopped trying to change
and control each other. and we are still working on
thinking long-term.

working to grow in compassion and decrease the
hold craving and aversion have over our behaviors
is essential, but we must also deal directly with the
systems and ideologies of harm that have emerged
from these conditions. our task as people of the
twenty-first century is to embrace the complexity
that is inherent in the experience of the individual
and of humanity. if we can embrace ourselves
deeply and take action on behalf of ourselves
and all beings, we will be able to reorganize the
world into a place where all can safely flourish and
exercise their power.

people working on their healing,
the ones with new love in their hearts,
more self-awareness in their minds,
a greater ability to manage their reactions,
who are actively undoing their patterns and
biases, are helping to create a better world.
your compassion creates real change.

you may ask yourself: which comes first—inner work or working to make the world a better place? the answer is that both can happen at the same time. we are all deeply imperfect and full of conditioning that clouds the mind. inner work is a lifelong journey, and so we should not wait until we get to the "end" of our healing to help others. practice your new habits and heal yourself while you work to undo oppression on a larger scale. moving against oppression is empathy becoming one with action.

the inner work we do supports the larger movement toward a better world. each makes the other stronger. inner work helps us rise above our old conditioning so that we decrease the harm we recreate in our interactions. the outer work of collective action makes compassion structural—it helps us build a world where people can feel safe and have their material needs met without directly or indirectly harming one another. self-awareness that becomes collective action is the medicine this earth needs.

real communication happens when projections
cease and we are willing to listen to each other
in a selfless manner. this becomes more possible
when we engage with ourselves deeply, actively
work on healing our old pain and trauma, and
become familiar with our patterns. the more we
know ourselves, the better we can come to know
those around us. communication is critical to any
movement—it is how we focus our power and
collectively decide our direction.

three sources of hurt:

attachment

expectation

judgment

three sources of healing:

compassion

commitment

observation

part of knowing yourself
is taking the time to understand
the society in which you live

the direct and indirect messages
you absorb as you grow up
quietly enter the mind
and harden into conditioning
that affects your perspective

without knowing
you develop implicit biases

without critical analysis
the past takes root in your thinking

without awareness and love
it is hard to live compassionately

it is up to us to envision and enact a new standard
for society, to deeply realize the value of human life
so that the compassionate treatment of all people
becomes the guiding principle that dictates how we
design our communities, institutions, and nations.

our world has fallen into extremes. greed,
competition, individualism, and short-sighted
decision-making have created a world of plenty
for some and a world of struggle for most. we are
out of balance. we live within systems that push
against each other and easily cause direct and
indirect forms of harm. we do not yet know how to
win together or how to live well without damaging
our earth.

fortunately, humanity is in the process of maturing.
we are young, but we are more open to learning,
growing, and reorganizing our world than ever
before. *it is up to us to make compassion structural.*
to create an inclusive society in which people are
not left behind because of their differences but
embraced and centered so that all can flourish.

it is undeniable that we can improve our current
global situation. to get to a better tomorrow, we
must understand the complexity of today. the
deeper our understanding, the clearer our actions.
we must come to terms with history; face it
directly without turning away. we must examine
where the shadows of history produce present-day
oppression. if we can accept the present reality of
human experience, we can better position ourselves
to undo structures that do not serve the common
good.

the forces of racism and heteropatriarchy exist on
the interpersonal and structural level. they impact
our institutions and insidiously slow down the flow
of compassion in our minds. we need to question
our current economic system and support a greater
distribution of material prosperity. none of our
systems will last forever; nothing does. starvation,
poverty, lack of access to good schooling and
healthcare are structural problems that we can
overcome—raising the standard so that people
no longer suffer on the material level is not an
impossibility; it is just a matter of will. collectively,
we have the wealth and knowledge to accomplish
this. what we are missing is a greater sense of
unconditional compassion. society will never be
perfect, but that should not stop us from making
our shared reality more humane. when we commit
to ending harm and supporting one another's
thriving, all individuals benefit.

our task is to think and act more collectively
while supporting the freedom of the individual. to
standardize the humane treatment of all people.
to expand our idea of human rights to include
economic empowerment. to dream and act big. to
be the leaders we wish existed.

we have the power to reorganize the world and
make compassion structural.

imagine a world where love guides society

people would not be hungry or in danger
bodies would feel safe and minds fully nourished
voices would be heard and differences respected

disputes would be handled
without violence or terror
everyone would have access
to the things they need to flourish

sharing
listening
telling the truth
not harming each other
being kind to one another
cleaning up after ourselves

essential lessons we were taught as small children
would be taken to heart by adults and woven into a
new global culture

meet those you encounter with genuine
compassion. live with intentional gentleness.
cultivate peace with your hands and words. be
generous with your kindness. allow others to share
in the bounty of a heart that dedicates itself to
goodwill. these are marvels of the human spirit,
actions that are most easily taken by healed hearts.
not only do these ways of being help our minds
settle into inner peace, but they create safer spaces
in a world that is always moving in and out of
turmoil. to bring such goodness into the world will
benefit many and bring its own countless rewards.

it is to the benefit of your inner peace
not to harm others

let this truth settle into your mind
and awaken when things get tough

when you think
revenge will calm your heart
or erase the pain you have felt

remember

when you think
spreading the turmoil you feel
will ease the fire burning inside of you

remember

when you think
making life harder for someone else
will avenge your pain

remember

it is to the benefit of your inner peace
not to harm others

let this truth settle into your mind
and awaken when things get tough

sending love to all

about the author

diego perez was born in ecuador and immigrated
to the united states as a child. he grew up in
boston and attended wesleyan university. during
a silent vipassana meditation course in 2012, he
saw that real healing and liberation were possible.
he became more committed to his meditation
practice while living in new york city. the results
he witnessed firsthand moved him to describe his
experiences in writing.

the penname yung pueblo means "young people"
and is meant to convey that humanity is entering
an era of remarkable growth and healing, when
many will expand their self-awareness and release
old burdens.

diego's online presence as yung pueblo, as well as
his books, *inward* and *clarity & connection*, are
meant to serve those undertaking their own journey
of personal transformation.

today, diego resides in western massachusetts with
his wife, where they live quietly and meditate daily.

Andrews McMeel Publishing
a division of Andrews McMeel Universal
1130 Walnut Street, Kansas City, Missouri 64106

www.andrewsmcmeel.com

21 22 23 24 25 RR4 10 9 8 7 6 5 4

ISBN: 978-1-5248-6048-6

Library of Congress Control Number: 2021931878

ATTENTION: SCHOOLS AND BUSINESSES

Andrews McMeel books are available at quantity discounts with bulk purchase for educational, business, or sales promotional use. For information, please e-mail the Andrews McMeel Publishing Special Sales Department: specialsales@amuniversal.com.